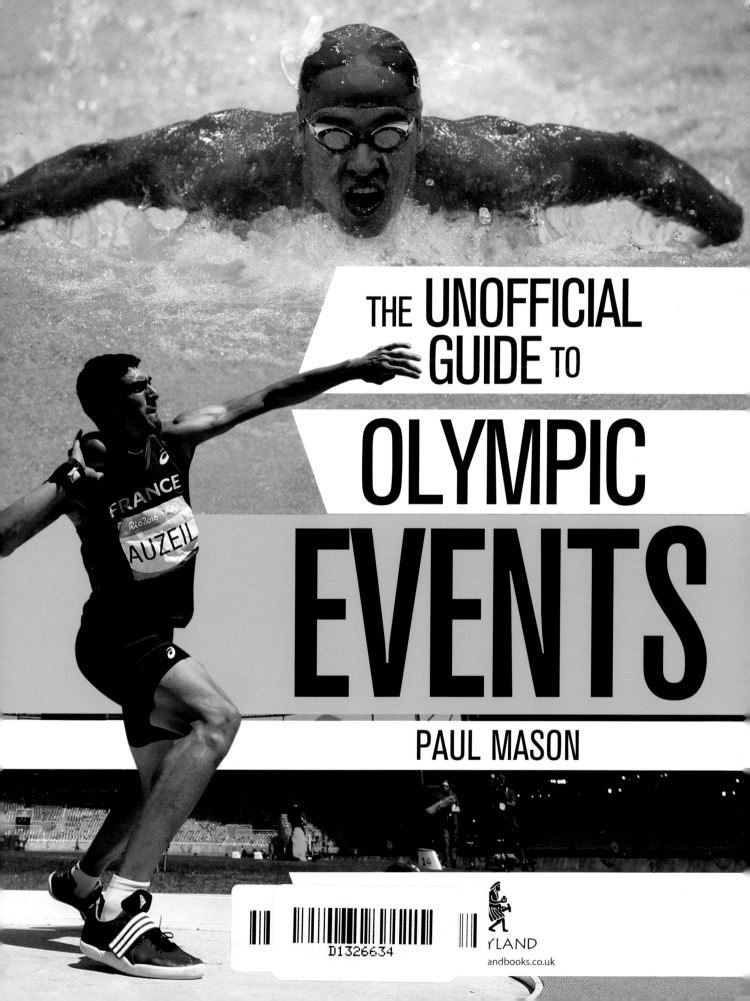

THE UNOFFICIAL GUIDE TO OLYMPIC EVENTS

PAUL MASON

YLAND
andbooks.co.uk

First published in 2019 by Wayland
Copyright © Hodder & Stoughton, 2019

Wayland
An imprint of
Hachette Children's Group
Part of Hodder and Stoughton
Carmelite House
50 Victoria Embankment
London EC4Y 0DZ

www.hachette.co.uk

Editor: Julia Bird
Design: RockJaw Creative

HB ISBN: 978 1 5263 1020 0
PB ISBN: 978 1 5263 1019 4

Printed in Dubai

MIX
Paper from
responsible sources
FSC
www.fsc.org
FSC® C104740

Please note: The statistics in this book were correct at the time of printing, but because of the nature of sport, it cannot be guaranteed that they are now accurate.

Picture credits: Diego Azubel/EPA/REX/Shutterstock: 9t. Bettmann Archive/Getty Images: 4-5b. Clive Brunskill/Getty Images: 24. CP DC Press/Shutterstock: 4cl. Droopydoganja/Dreamstime: 28. Franck Fife/AFP/Getty Images: 8. Marc Francotte/Corbis via Getty Images: 18. Alexander Hassenstein/Getty Images: front cover b, 1b. Andy Hooper/ANL/REX/Shutterstock: 7b. Patrick B Kraemer/REX/Shutterstock: 28. Antonio Lacerda/EPA/REX/Shutterstock: 23.Leswrona/Dreamstime; 22. Matthew Lewis/Getty Images: 7t. Alex Livesey/Getty Images: 21. Donald Miralle/Getty Images: 29. Dean Mouhtaropoulos/Getty Images: 14. Joern Pollex/FIFA via Getty Images: 19. Popperfoto/Getty Images: 13. Adam Pretty/Getty Images: front cover t, 1t. Celso Pupo/Dreamstime: 11t, 11b. REX/Shutterstock: 9b.Rka photography/Dreamstime: 17t. Dave Shopland/BPI/REX/Shutterstock: 10, 20. Sipa USA REX/Shutterstock: 2, 12, 17b. Stockphoto mania/Shutterstock: 5t. Petr Toman/Shutterstock: 15t. Topfoto: 8. Tim de Waele/Getty Images: 16. Xinhua/REX/Shutterstock: 27. Leonard Zhukovsky/Shutterstock: 3, 15b, 25.

Every attempt has been made to clear copyright. Should there be any inadvertent omission please apply to the publisher for rectification.

CONTENTS

The changing Olympics   4

Athletics (track)   6

Athletics (field)   8

Ball sports   10

Boat sports   12

Combat sports   14

Cycling   16

Football   18

Gymnastics   20

Multi-sport events   22

Racquet sports   24

Swimming and aquatics   26

New sports   28

Olympic events   30

Olympic words   31

Index and further information   32

The changing Olympics

At the very first ancient Olympics in 776 BCE there was just one event: a race called the stadion. It was won by a cook called Coroebus. More events were added later, until the final ancient Olympics was held in CE 393.

Above: A group of runners comes round the bend during a semi-final of the 1,500 metres at the 2016 Rio Olympics.

BIGGEST SPORTS AT THE 2020 OLYMPICS

These seven sports have the greatest number of events at the 2020 Games, according to the IOC:

Aquatics	49	Gymnastics	18
Athletics	48	Canoeing	16
Cycling	22	Judo	15
Wrestling	18		

Growth of the Games

In 1896, a new version of the Olympics was held, with 43 different events. Ever since, the list of events at the Summer Olympics has been getting longer. At the 2020 Olympics there will be 33 different sports and 339 events. (There are also over 100 Winter Olympic events – but there isn't space for them in this book!)

Some sports have only a small number of events. In football, for example, there are two: one each for men's and women's teams. Other sports have a lot more. Athletics is one of the biggest, with 25 track events, 16 field, 5 road and 2 multi-sport.

Forgotten events: shooting

The shooting at today's Olympics is nothing like some of the shooting events in 1900, when the Games were held in Paris.

Back then, instead of shooting at clay pigeons the competitors shot at live ones. The birds were released from traps in front of the shooters, who had to kill as many pigeons as possible. A shooter who missed two in a row left the competition. In total nearly 300 pigeons were killed.

The use of live targets was banned in 1902 and at the 1904 Games, clay pigeons were used.

Eek!

Changing events

The events at the Olympics change from one Olympic Games to the next. Old events, such as the tug-of-war, are regularly dropped from the Olympics, while new sports are added. The International Olympic Committee (IOC) has decided to keep core sports such as athletics and swimming at every Olympic Games. There is also space for 'guest' sports that are suggested by the host country.

Below: 1920, Antwerp: the USA and Great Britain battle it out in the quarter-finals of the tug-of-war. Great Britain won 2–0 and went on to win gold.

Athletics (track)

Track events are mostly running races, though sometimes they also involve jumping over barriers. They are usually separated into sprint, middle-distance and long-distance races.

There's a full list of all the Olympic events on page 30.

100 metres

The 100 metres race is the biggest sprint event, and probably the most watched event at the whole Olympics. The racers use starting blocks. When the gun goes, they stay low for the first seven or eight strides, looking down at the track. They power forward using their elbows and legs until they come upright at about 30 metres. From here to about 60 metres they accelerate to maximum speed. They then try to slow down as little as possible the rest of the way to the finishing line.

Below: Jamaica's Elaine Thompson wins the women's 100 metres at the 2016 Olympics. In third was another Jamaican, Shelly-Ann Fraser-Pryce, who had won gold in 2008 and 2012.

4 x 400 metres mixed relay

This was introduced as a new event for Tokyo 2020. Teams have two men and two women, each running a lap of the track. They can run in any order: because men are faster than women, the lead often changes hands several times before the end.

1,500 metres

The 1,500 metres is probably the most popular middle-distance race at the Olympics. The athletes have to combine speed with endurance. Runners with good endurance may try to go fast from the start and leave everyone behind. Those with a fast finish try to stick behind them, then win the sprint down the finishing straight.

5k and 10k

On track, the two long-distance races are the 5k (or 5,000 metres) and 10k (10,000 metres). They suit lightweight runners with superhuman endurance, so the same athletes often take part in both races.

Above right: *In a relay race, each runner has to pass the baton to the next while inside a designated part of the track. If they fail, or drop it, they are disqualified.*

Below: *Long-distance running legend Mo Farah collects another Olympic gold.*

EXPLAINER: **MIXED EVENTS**

Mixed events are team races with the teams made up of men and women in equal numbers. For the 2020 Olympics, mixed events were added to four sports:

▶ 4 x 400 metres relay in athletics
▶ 4 x 100 metres medley relay in swimming
▶ A mixed triathlon relay *(see page 22)*
▶ Mixed doubles in table tennis

FAMOUS WINS: **FARAH'S** FOURTH

In 2012, Great Britain's Mo Farah won the 5k and 10k races at his home Games. In 2016, at the Rio Olympics, he won the 10k. Could Mo win his last race, the 5k, before he retired from the track?

With 200 metres to go, it looked unlikely. Farah was in the lead, but his opponents were queuing up on his shoulder, waiting to sprint past. Then, heading into the last 100 metres, Farah attacked. No one could catch him: he crossed the line first, Olympic champion for a fourth time.

Athletics (field)

There are two key types of field event: speed-based ones such as the long jump and pole vault, and power-based ones such as the discus and hammer throw.

Long jump

The long jump is the only field event with a crossover to track athletics. This event is all about speed. The jumpers sprint down the runway, plant their foot on the board at the end, and leap up and forward. As long as they get the technique correct, more speed produces a longer jump.

High jump

It would be hard to mistake an Olympic high-jumper for anything else. They must be among the tallest and thinnest athletes at the Games. Being tall makes it easier to get over a higher bar. So does being light!

Javelin

The javelin throw is one of the oldest Olympic events. At the modern Games javelin was first included for men in 1908 and for women in 1932.

The thrower takes a run-up before turning sideways so that the javelin trails behind. He or she stops suddenly and whips the javelin-holding arm through before letting go. Usually at this point the thrower lets loose a massive bellow or scream!

Left: Two great US athletes have won gold at long jump and 100 metres at the same Games: Jesse Owens (shown here) in 1936, and Carl Lewis in 1984 and 1988. Lewis also won the long jump in 1992 and 1996.

Right: The athlete has to throw the javelin without touching or crossing the white line. Otherwise it is a 'foul throw' and the distance will not count.

FAMOUS WINS:
FOSBURY FLOPS

Until the 1960s most high-jumpers used a technique called the straddle jump. They took off and used the leg furthest from the bar to add height to the jump, then pivoted over the bar belly- down.

At the 1968 Olympics, a US jumper called Dick Fosbury used a new high-jumping style. Fosbury went over with his back to the bar, head and shoulders leading. Then he flopped down onto the landing mat. Fosbury won gold – and his Fosbury Flop technique spread around the world.

Above: *Mutaz Essa Barshim of Qatar midway through a Dick Fosbury-inspired high jump at the 2016 Rio Olympics.*

EXPLAINER:
QUALIFIERS AND FINALS

▶ In Olympic field athletics, every competitor takes part in a qualifying round to decide who goes through to the final.

▶ In discus, javelin, shot put and hammer, for example, everyone gets three throws. The twelve athletes with the longest throws go through.

▶ In the final, the scores are wiped clean. There are six more rounds of throwing to decide the winner. They go in reverse order, with the top-placed qualifier going last in each round, before the winner is finally decided.

Ball sports

Ball sports at the Olympics include rugby sevens, football, handball, hockey, golf and two types of volleyball. You can find out about Olympic football on page 18.

Rugby sevens

Rugby is a new-old Olympic sport. The 15-a-side version was last played at the Games in 1924. Ninety-two years later, rugby sevens appeared at the 2016 Rio Olympics.

Sevens gets its name from there being seven players per team, with each half lasting seven minutes*. Matches are held on a full-size pitch, so there is plenty of space to run without being tackled: the ball moves quickly and there are often lots of tries. The action is almost non-stop and players only get a two-minute break at half time, so they have to be extremely fit.

*In the final match, the halves last 10 minutes.

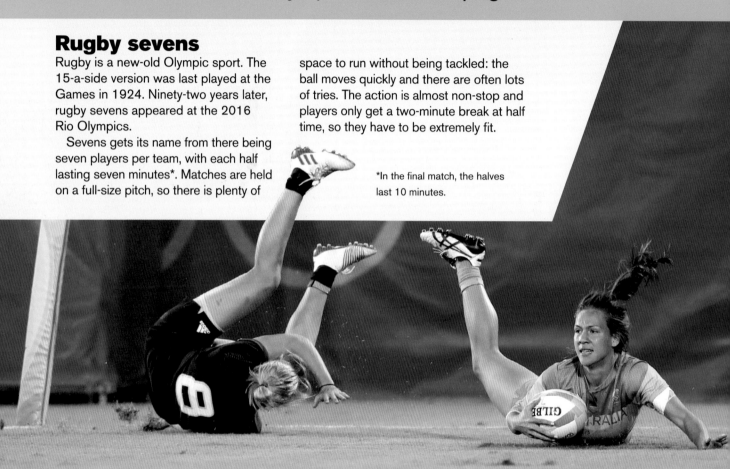

EXPLAINER: **SEVENS POINTS**

In rugby sevens, points can be scored in four ways:

► A try (5 points), touching the ball down in the in-goal area past the goalposts
► A conversion (2 points), for kicking the ball through the posts after a try
► A penalty (3 points), for kicking the ball through the posts after a foul by the other team
► A drop-goal (3 points), for kicking the ball through the posts during normal play.

Above: *Australia play New Zealand in the rugby sevens final at the 2016 Olympics. Australia won and became the first women's champions. Fiji beat Great Britain to win the men's gold.*

Handball

Handball is all action: there are a lot of goals, sometimes 50 or more in a match. It is also quite physical, with lots of barging and grappling. Referees often play advantage and let the game continue after fouls.

Players must hold the ball in their hand for no more than three seconds and can only take three steps with it. They cannot go into the 'inner D', the goalkeeper's area, except by jumping into it to shoot (they must shoot before landing). The goalkeeper can hold the ball for longer and touch it with any part of his or her body.

Left: Germany play France in the 2016 Olympic handball tournament. French player Mathieu Grébille (in white) is a step away from the goalkeeper's area.

Above: At the 2016 Olympics, Brazil was hoping to copy the USA in 2008, and win both men's and women's beach volleyball contests. The men's team took gold; the women's team had to be happy with silver.

Beach volleyball

Beach volleyball is played outdoors on a sandy court, with two players per team. The ball is inflated to be softer than in the indoor game and travels more slowly (in indoor volleyball it can reach over 130 kph). Matches last three sets. In the first two sets, the first team to score 21 points wins. In the last set the first team to 15 wins.

Boat sports

At the Olympics there are two basic kinds of boat: ones you have to row or paddle and ones that are blown along by the wind*.

*There's also one event without an actual boat at all: windsurfing.

The eight

The eight is one of the most exciting events at the Olympic rowing regatta. It is the only coxed race, with a cox in the back of the boat steering the rowers. The eight is a 'sweep' event, with rowers holding one oar with both hands.

Each rower has to combine extreme fitness and strength with good technique. Unless their strokes are well timed and the same length, they risk clashing oars, catching water or going off course.

Windsurfing

This is the oddball among the sailing events: it is the only one you stand up for, and the only one that doesn't involve a boat. Windsurfers are smaller and more manoeuverable than other sailing craft at the Games. The races are often close tactical battles, carried out at high speeds.

Below: There are two types of slalom event. In kayak or K events, the paddle has a blade at each end. In canoe or C ones, the paddle is shorter with one blade.

Canoe slalom

This is a crowd-pleasing event. It's impossible to take your eyes off the paddlers: at any moment they could be swept away!

The aim is to paddle down a whitewater course as quickly as possible. The competitors must pass through 20 gates – pairs of poles hanging down over the water – without touching them. Touching a gate adds two seconds to your time; missing one completely adds 50 seconds. Some gates have to be taken in an upstream direction, which usually involves sudden changes of direction and some furious paddling.

In sailing contests, the winner gets one point, second place two, etc. After ten races, the ten sailors with the fewest points go through to the final race.

The final race has double points, so losing is doubly serious. At the end, the gold medal goes to the sailor with the fewest points in total.

Below: *In order from front to back, Matthew Pinsent, Tim Foster, Steve Redgrave and James Cracknell.*

FAMOUS WINS:
REDGRAVE'S FIVE

Great Britain's coxed four at the 2000 Sydney Olympics included a legendary rower: Steve Redgrave. Redgrave had won gold at the last four Olympic Games, starting back in 1984. Winning one more – at the age of 38 – would make him the most successful Olympic rower ever.

In the final, Great Britain led with Italy, Australia and Slovenia close behind. Near the finish Italy attacked and caught up – but Redgrave and the rest held on, winning by less than half a second.

"Self-belief is probably the most crucial factor in sporting success. It's the iron in the mind … that wins medals." – Steve Redgrave

Combat sports

Combat sports have been part of the Olympics since ancient times. One of them, wrestling, has been at the Games since the 700s BCE.

Boxing

In boxing there are five events for women and eight for men, so 13 in total. In the past, the men's super-heavyweight event has been among the most attention-grabbing. Several super-heavyweight gold medallists have later won professional world titles, including Lennox Lewis, Wladimir Klitschko and Anthony Joshua.

Below: Since 2012 women have been allowed to box at the Olympics. The first ever female gold medallist, Nicola Adams (in red), went on to win a second gold at Rio 2016.

EXPLAINER:
SCORES IN BOXING

Boxers are given scores by judges at the end of each round. They decide who has won based on how many good punches each boxer has thrown, how aggressive he or she has been and whether good boxing technique has been used.

The winner gets 10 points and the loser gets a number less than 10. At the end of the fight, the boxer with the most points wins.

EXPLAINER:
WEIGHT DIVISIONS

Events for all combat sports (except fencing) are divided into weight divisions. In boxing, for example, female fighters weighing 51–57 kg are in the featherweight division. This system gives smaller fighters a chance to win medals and makes boxing safer.

EXPLAINER:
GRECO-ROMAN V FREESTYLE

In Greco-Roman wrestling, the players can only use their upper body and arms to throw and pin down their opponent. In Freestyle wrestling, any part of the body can be used, including the legs.

Judo

In judo, players can win by throwing or pinning their opponent down. Ippon, the highest score, ends a contest. Waza-ari is a lower score: two waza-ari equal ippon and also end the match. Yuko is the lowest score: if the match runs out of time, the player with most yuko wins.

Until 2020, judo at the Olympics was an individual contest. For the Tokyo 2020 Games, though, a team contest was introduced.

Right: In judo, a perfect throw, with the opponent landing completely on their back, will score ippon and end the contest.

Wrestling

Wrestling was part of the ancient Olympics and there has been wrestling at every modern Games. So it was a shock when, in 2013, the IOC decided to cut wrestling from the Games.

Former medallists returned their medals in protest. One top wrestling coach even went on hunger strike. Wrestling changed its rules to make contests faster and more action-packed, and added new events for women. In response, the IOC put wrestling back on the Olympic programme.

Left: A Greco-Roman wrestling contest between Hungary's Peter Bacsi and Carlos Andres Muñoz Jaramillo of Colombia.

Cycling

There are four different kinds of cycling at the Olympics: track, road, BMX and mountain bike. Track cycling has most events, with six.

Keirin

This event probably takes the prize for the hottest ticket at the 2020 Tokyo Olympics. Keirin was invented in Japan and is massively popular there. At the start the riders fight for position, before settling into a line behind the 'derny' motorbike. By the time they reach the last laps, the riders are going full speed within a few centimetres of one another: watch out for some spectacular crashes.

EXPLAINER: **KEIRIN RULES**

The riders follow a motorbike called a derny for five-and-a-half laps. It steadily goes faster until it reaches 50 kph, then it leaves the track. The cyclists must not pass the back wheel of the derny until it is off the track. (If they misjudge it, the race starts again.) Then the cyclists race each other for another two-and-a-half laps.

Road time trial

In most cycling races you can slipstream behind other riders to save energy, have better tactics than your rivals or get help from teammates. Not in the time trial. Riders set off one at a time, with the same gap between each. The one who pedals to the finish in the fastest time wins.

Left: Because only the strongest rider will win, the road time trial is sometimes called the race of truth.

Below: In a BMX race like this one from the 2016 Olympics, the rider who clears the first jump ahead of the pack always has a good chance of winning.

Opposite: Riders from Germany, Australia, Great Britain and the Netherlands (four of the powerhouse teams in track cycling) line up behind the derny during the London 2012 Games.

BMX freestyle

BMX freestyle was first chosen as a cycling event for the 2020 Olympics. Each rider does two one-minute runs in a contest area full of ramps (it looks a lot like a giant-sized skatepark). The aim is to impress the judges with as many spectacular jumps, spins, flips etc. as possible. The riders get points for the difficulty, originality, style, flow, risk, height and execution of their tricks.

Mountain bike

Mountain biking first appeared at the Olympics in 1996. Back then the course was fairly dull, without many challenges for the riders. Things have now changed and the riders have to cope with tricky uphill zigzags, drop-offs, downhill steps, rock gardens and other obstacles.

Football

There has been some sort of football tournament at almost every Olympics since 1900*, although some people say the first *real* competition was in 1908.

*Los Angeles in 1932 did not have football. This was also the only Olympics at which American football appeared, as a demonstration sport.

Early days

Some people claim a match was played at the first ever modern Olympics in 1896, but no medals were awarded. By 1900 football was definitely part of the Olympics. It was played by scratch teams or club sides, rather than full international teams. In 1900, for example, 'Great Britain' won – but the team was actually the London club Upton Park F.C.

"As there is a month to go before we leave for Berlin, kindly take some exercise." – The head of the British Olympic Association in a letter to the team's footballers, just before the 1936 Olympics

Below: Romario, of Brazil, chases the ball at the 1988 Olympics. Despite his efforts Brazil lost 2-1 to the USSR in the final.

The world's biggest tournament

From 1908 onwards, Olympic football was played by full international teams chosen from each country's best players. By the 1920s, the Olympics was the world's biggest international competition. The best team at this time was Uruguay, which won in 1924 and 1928. Football's governing body, FIFA, held the first World Cup in 1930 – Uruguay won that, too.

Women's football

A hundred years after the start of the modern Olympics, women were allowed to play football at the Games for the first time. The USA won the tournament in 1996.

Olympic football today

Today the men's competition is for 16 teams and the women's is for 12. The teams play in groups of four and all the teams in the group play each other. They get three points for a win, one point for a draw and none for losing. The top two teams in each group (plus the two best third-place finishers in the women's tournament) advance to the knockout rounds. These are the quarter- and semi-finals, followed by the gold- and bronze-medal matches.

FAMOUS WINS: NORWAY BEAT GERMANY, 1936

In 1936 the Olympics were held in Berlin, Germany. When Germany beat Luxembourg 9–0, the country's leader Adolf Hitler decided to go along to their next game. Hitler and the other Nazi Party leaders left with red faces, though. Their team LOST, 2–0 to Norway.

Hitler apparently never watched a football match again.

Right: Football on day one of the Rio 2016 Games, and Alex Morgan of the USA sprints for the ball during the match against France.

Gymnastics

Gymnastics is one of the big draws at the Olympics. There are three different kinds: artistic, rhythmic and trampolining.

Below: Amy Tinkler of Great Britain midway through her floor exercise at Rio 2016. Her routine was good enough to win a bronze medal.

Floor exercise

This is one of the most popular artistic gymnastics events. Gymnasts perform a 90-second routine that has to include certain skills. Women's routines include tumbling and dance moves, while men have to include tumbling and strength moves. Women's routines are set to music the gymnast has chosen and must finish in time with it.

Vault

The vault is a super-fast event. It is so quick that it is hard to see what the gymnast has done, until the TV plays it back in slow motion. The judges are looking for good body position during the entire vault, a strong exit from the vault table and a controlled landing.

Left: European champion Oleg Verniaiev of Ukraine vaults at the Rio Games. Verniaiev came fifth in vault, but won on the parallel bars.

EXPLAINER: **SCORING**

Gymnasts get a score based on two numbers:

▶ Their difficulty score, based on the skills they perform. Trying harder skills earns you a higher difficulty score. Top gymnasts have difficulty scores of 6–7 for women and 6.5–7.5 for men.

▶ Their execution score, based on how well they perform the skills. The best execution score you could get would be 10, but the judges almost always knock off points for errors. Scores over 9 are very rare in everything except the vault.

Forgotten events

There were quite a few unusual gymnastics events at the early modern Olympics. Rope climbing was popular and so was an event called club swinging.
  Strangest of all was possibly the team competition, which was very different from the modern version. In 1912, teams had to have between 16 and 40 gymnasts. They performed a routine of movements all together – like a sort of gymnastics line dancing.

All-round

This is a contest for gymnasts who are great at every event – because it includes every event. The scores from each one are added together. For the women there are four events (beam, floor, uneven bars and balance beam). The men have six (floor, high bar, parallel bars, pommel horse, rings and vault).

Multi-sport events

For some athletes, being good at only one event just isn't hard enough. They want to compete at three, five, seven or even ten different events before deciding who's best.

Triathlon

The triathlon course is always chosen to make the host city look great, and the sight of triathletes swimming, biking and running their way around draws a big audience.

In all three sports it is easiest to go fast in a small group working together. The tactics of who works with whom are constantly changing. A weaker swimmer might want to draft behind someone faster. On the bike leg or run, though, it might be better to leave them behind.

The 2020 Tokyo Olympics include the mixed relay triathlon for the first time. Two women and two men make up a team. They each do a short triathlon before handing over to the next triathlete.

EXPLAINER:
TRI TRANSITION

The area where athletes change from one sport to another is called transition. From swimming to cycling is called T1. The racers strip off their wetsuit (if they are wearing one), collect their bike and run to the exit. They cannot ride their bike until they have left the transition zone.

The racers come back to the zone for T2 after the bike section. They dismount before entering, park the bike, put on their running shoes and race off.

Above: *In triathlon the athletes swim 1.5 km, cycle 40 km and run 10 km. In the triathlon relay each does a 300 metre swim, 8 km bike and 2 km run.*

Opposite: *Kevin Mayer of France ahead of Ashton Eaton of the USA in the 2016 decathlon hurdles. Eaton went on to win the decathlon, repeating his gold medal win of 2012.*

Heptathlon and decathlon

These are athletics events that mix strength, endurance and sprinting. Few athletes are good at all three. A good javelin thrower, for example, might be OK at sprinting, but not so good at 1,500 metres running. Over the course of two days' competition, the best all-round athlete emerges as the winner.

Racquet sports

There are three racquet sports at the Olympics – although one of them doesn't really use a racquet*. They are tennis, badminton and table tennis.

Tennis

Men's singles (singles tennis has one player on each side of the net) was part of the Olympics in 1896. Four years later women were allowed to play as well. In 1928, though, tennis dropped off the list of Olympic sports and only reappeared 60 years later, in 1988.

Many of the world's top players now compete at the Olympic tournament. It has been won by greats such as Serena and Venus Williams, Andy Murray and Rafa Nadal. The matches are usually played on a hard court, but are sometimes on clay or grass.

Below: *Serena and Venus Williams (left and right) of the USA. The sisters won Olympics tennis doubles golds in 2000, 2008 and 2012.*

* Table tennis uses a thing that's called a racquet, but it is made of solid material. Racquets are usually made of a frame with fibre strung across it.

FAMOUS VICTORY: **MURRAY'S** DOUBLE

In 2012, Andy Murray won the singles tennis title at his home Olympics. It was a good year for Murray, who had won Wimbledon (one of the world's biggest pro tournaments) weeks before.

At the 2016 Olympics the tennis was played on a hard court. It suited Murray less than the grass courts of 2012. Even so he fought through to the final, where he beat Juan Martín del Potro.

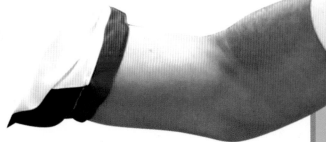

Left: Andy Murray on his way to winning in the 2016 Olympics. The victory made him the first player ever to win two Olympic singles titles.

Badminton

Badminton is played by men and women, in singles (with one player each side of the net), doubles (two players) and mixed doubles (a male and a female player). The game was invented in the 1870s, but it first appeared as a full Olympic sport only in 1992. Badminton is very popular in Asian countries and they often dominate. In fact, between 1992 and 2008, Asian athletes won 69 of the 76 available badminton medals.

Swimming and aquatics

The four aquatic sports at the Olympics are swimming (which includes marathon swimming), diving, synchronised swimming and water polo.

Below: In a freestyle race the swimmers can do any stroke they like. Everyone does front crawl, though, because it is fastest.

50 metre freestyle

This is the equivalent of the 100 metres in track athletics: the winner gets to say they were the fastest man or woman in the pool. The men take about 35 strokes to do 50 metres, the women about 38. Usually the swimmers don't breathe until they have finished!

4 x 100 metres mixed medley relay

This is a new event for 2020. Teams contain two men and two women. The race is swum backstroke, breaststroke, butterfly and front crawl. The teams have to work out their overall fastest combination of male and female swimmers. The lead can change several times and there are often dramatic finishes.

Forgotten events

The strangest event at early Olympics was probably the swimming obstacle course at the 1900 Paris Games. It involved climbing over a pole, then over a row of boats, then swimming under a row of boats.

The same Games also had an underwater-swimming event. Unsurprisingly this was not very interesting to watch and never appeared at the Olympics again.

10-metre diving

As anyone who has stood at the edge of a 10-metre diving platform will tell you, this is one of the scariest events in the pool. The water seems a VERY long way down.

In the final, women do five dives and the men six. Each dive is scored out of ten by the judges. The judges' scores are then multiplied by a difficulty score, a number representing how hard the dive is. Only the best dives score over 100, even in an Olympic final.

Right: *From the 10-metre platform it takes three seconds to hit the water. By then the divers are travelling at 50 kph.*

"Once every four years, you get a chance to compete in the Olympics. You have these six dives that decide whether you're an Olympic medallist or not – which is quite intense."
– Tom Daley, two-time Olympic bronze medallist

New sports

For the 2020 Olympics, five new sports have been added to the Games. They are baseball/softball, climbing, karate, skateboarding and surfing.

"I am delighted that the Olympic Games in Tokyo [2020] will be more youthful, more urban and will include more women." – IOC president Thomas Bach, 2017

New sports and events, 2020 Olympics:

SPORTS	EVENTS (there are male and female versions unless stated)
Baseball/softball	Six-team baseball tournament for men, six-team softball tournament for women
Karate	Kata Kumite (three weight divisions)
Skateboarding	Street Park
Sport climbing	Bouldering Lead Speed combined
Surfing	Shortboard

Baseball/softball
Baseball and softball have similar rules. Both are very popular in North America and Asia. Softball has been played at the Olympics before, between 1996 and 2008. USA won gold the first four times, but Japan won in 2008 – making them the reigning Olympic champions until 2020 when softball reappears at the games.

Karate
There will be two different karate events in 2020. The first is kumite, where opponents fight for a set time (two minutes for women, three for men). You win by getting eight points more than your opponent, or having more points at the end.

The second karate event is kata. This is not a fight. Instead, athletes take turns to demonstrate specific techniques. The winner is the one the judges think performed them best.

Below: The key difference between softball and baseball is that in softball, the pitcher has to throw underarm.

Below: Brighton Zeuner, the youngest skater ever to win an X Games gold medal (she was only 13) and a pre-Games favourite for women's skateboarding gold at the 2020 Olympics.

Skateboarding

The street skateboarding course features stairs, handrails, curbs, benches, walls and slopes. Each skater does a range of tricks, and the judges give scores depending on difficulty, height, speed, originality and execution.

In park, the course is made up of a range of bowls hollowed out of the ground. The skaters launch themselves high above the lip to perform aerials, so this is a spectacular event to watch.

Surfing

Surfing will be a big draw at the Olympics, as it is popular around the world. Australia, Brazil and the USA have the highest numbers of top-level surfers. France, Japan, Portugal and others also have top contenders.

At the Olympics surfers will compete in groups of four. They can catch as many waves as they like, but only their top two scores count. At the end, the two with the highest total scores go through to the next round.

Climbing

There are three climbing events, but the fastest, most exciting one is speed climbing. Two climbers race each other up a 15-metre wall, set at an overhanging angle of 95 degrees. The best male climbers take 5–6 seconds to reach the top, the best females 7–8 seconds.

Olympic events

Adventure/street sports: skateboarding park, street; sport climbing bouldering, lead, speed combined; surfing shortboard

Aquatic sports: diving 3m springboard, 10m platform, synchronised 3m springboard, synchronised 10m platform; swimming 50m, 100m, 200m, 400m, 800m and 1500m freestyle, 100m and 200m backstroke, 100m and 200m breaststroke, 100m and 200m butterfly, 200m and 400m individual medley, 4x100m and 2x200m freestyle relay, 4x100m medley relay, 4x100m mixed medley relay, 10k marathon swim (open water); synchronised swimming duets (women), teams (women); water polo 12-team tournament (men), 10-team tournament (women)

Athletics, track: 100m, 200m, 400m, 800m, 1,500m, 5,000m, 10,000m,110m hurdles (men), 100m hurdles (women), 400m hurdles, 3,000m steeplechase, 4 x 100m relay, 4 x 400m relay, 4 x 400m mixed relay

Athletics, field: high jump, pole vault, long jump, triple jump, shot put, discus, hammer, javelin

Ball sports: baseball (men)/softball (women), basketball, beach volleyball, football, golf, handball, hockey, rugby sevens, table tennis, tennis, volleyball

Boat sports

Canoe: slalom kayak single (K-1) and slalom canoe single (C-1), sprint kayak single (K-1) 200m, 500m (women), 1,000m (men), double (K-2) 500m (women), double (K-2) 1,000m (men), four (K-4) 500m, canoe single (C-1) 200m (women), canoe single (C-1) 1,000m (men), canoe double (C-2) 500m (women), canoe double (C-2) 1,000m (men)

Rowing: single sculls, pair, double sculls, four, quadruple sculls, eight, lightweight double sculls

Sailing: RS:X windsurfer, Laser 1-person dinghy (men), Laser Radial 1-person dinghy (women), Finn 1-person dinghy (heavyweight) (men), 470 2-person dinghy, 49er skiff (men), 49er FX skiff (women), Nacra 17 (mixed)

Combat sports

Boxing: in 2020 women fight in fly, feather, light, welter and middle-weight divisions; men in eight weight divisions, still to be confirmed

Fencing: individual foil, individual epée, individual sabre, team foil, team epée, team sabre

Judo: men under 60kg, 66kg, 73kg, 81kg, 90kg, 100kg and over 100kg; women under 48kg, 52kg, 57kg, 63kg, 70kg, 78kg and over 78kg; mixed team

Karate: kata, kumite

Taekwondo: men fight in up to 58kg, 68kg, 80kg and over 80kg, women in under 49kg, 57kg, 67kg and over 67kg

Wrestling: freestyle, men under 57kg, 65kg, 74kg, 86kg, 97kg and 125kg; freestyle, women under 48kg, 53kg, 58kg, 63kg, 69kg and 75kg; Greco-Roman, men under 59kg, 66kg, 75kg, 85kg, 98kg and 130kg

Cycling: BMX freestyle/park, BMX race; mountain bike cross-country; road race, individual time trial; track team sprint, sprint, keirin, team pursuit, omnium, madison

Equestrian sports: dressage (individual and team), eventing (individual and team), jumping (individual and team)

Gymnastics, artistic: team competition, individual all-round, floor exercise, vault, uneven bars (women), beam (women), rings (men), pommel horse (men), parallel bars (men), horizontal bar (men)

Gymnastics, rhythmic: individual all-round competition (women), group all-round competition (women)

Gymnastics, trampoline: individual competition

Multi-event sports: triathlon (individual swim/run/bike, mixed relay 2 x males and 2 x females); pentathlon (fencing, swimming, equestrian, shooting and running combined); decathlon (day 1: 100m, long jump, shot put, high jump, 400m; day 2: 110m hurdles, discus, pole vault, javelin, 1500m); heptathlon (day 1: 100m hurdles, high jump, shot put, 200m; day 2: long jump, javelin, 800m)

Racquet sports: tennis: singles, doubles, mixed doubles (one male, one female); table tennis: singles, team, mixed doubles (one male, one female); badminton: singles, doubles, mixed doubles (one male, one female)

Target sports: shooting 50m rifle 3 positions, 10m air rifle, 25m rapid fire pistol (men), 25m pistol (women), 10m air pistol, trap, skeet, 10m air rifle mixed team, 10m air pistol mixed team; trap mixed team; archery individual, team, mixed team

Weightlifting: females lift in under 48kg, 53kg, 58 kg, 63kg, 69kg, 75kg and over 75kg; males lift in seven categories that have not yet been confirmed

Olympic words

Advantage allowing play to carry on after an offence has been committed, to give the non-offending team a chance to score

Bar in high jump and pole vault, the bar is the long horizontal pole the jumpers must get over without it falling off

Cox in rowing, the person who guides the boat and gives instructions to the rowers

Demonstration sport a sport that is played at the Olympics as an experiment, without medals being awarded

Drop-off in mountain biking, a drop-off is a sudden, very steep downhill slope

Endurance ability to do something for a long time

Final last race or contest in an event, which decides the winner

Finishing straight straight path leading to the finish; on a running track, the finishing straight is 100 metres long

Hard court tennis court with a hard surface, such as concrete or asphalt

Heat first part of a contest, which decides which sportspeople will go through to the later stages

Host the country or city where an Olympic Games takes place

Hunger strike refusing to eat food, usually as a protest against something that is seen as unfair

IOC short for International Olympic Committee, the organisation that runs the Olympic Games

Knockout in sports, the knockout part of a contest is one where the loser or losers leave the competition

Medley swimming race using all four strokes. Individual medley races are swum butterfly, backstroke, breaststroke, freestyle; team races are backstroke, breaststroke, butterfly, freestyle

Open water any water that is not a swimming pool

Performance-enhancing drugs banned drugs, which allow sportspeople to do better than if they had not taken the drugs

Regatta sailing or rowing competition

Rock garden in mountain biking, a rock garden is an area where the ground is mostly made up of different-sized rocks. Rock gardens are bumpy and tricky to ride across

Round stage of a competition; for example, the third round of a boxing match is the third period of fighting

Scratch team team pulled together quickly, using whoever is available at the time

Slipstream shelter behind another competitor as a way of feeling less air resistance

Stroke in rowing, a stroke is one pull on the oar or oars, plus the return to the starting position for the next pull

Tactics plan for how to do something (such as win a race)

Tandem in cycling, a tandem is a bike ridden by two people

Try score in rugby, where the attacker crosses the other team's goal line and touches the ball to the ground

Vault table gymnastic equipment on which vaults are performed

Whitewater rough water that flows quickly downhill

Index

Adams, Nicola 14
aquatics 4–5, 26–27
athletics 4–8
    field 4, 8–9
    track 4, 6–8, 26

badminton 24–25
Barshim, Mutaz Essa 9
baseball 28
biking, mountain 16–17
boxing 14–15

canoeing 4, 12
climbing 28–29
cycling 4, 16–17, 22
    BMX freestyle 16–17

Daley, Tom 27
decathlon 22–23
diving 26–27

Eaton, Ashton 22–23

Farrah, Mo 7
football 4, 10, 18–19
Fosbury, Dick 9

gymnastics 4, 20–21
handball 10–11

heptathlon 23

International Olympic
Committee (IOC) 4–5,
    15, 28

javelin 8–9
judo 4, 15
jumps, long/high 8–9

karate 28
keirin 16

Lewis, Carl 8

Mayer, Kevin 22–23
Murray, Andy 24–25

Olympics, ancient 4, 14–15
Owens, Jesse 8

Redgrave, Steve 13
relays, running 7
rowing 12–13
rugby sevens 10
running 4, 6–7, 22

sailing 12–13
shooting 5

skateboarding 28–29
softball 28
stadion 4
surfing 28–29
swimming 4–5, 22, 26–27

table tennis 7, 24
tennis 24–25
Thompson, Elaine 6
throws 8–9
Tinkler, Amy 20
triathlon 7, 22–23
tug-of-war 5

vault, pole 8–9
Verniaiev, Oleg 21
volleyball, beach 10–11

water polo 26
Williams, Serena 24
    Venus 24
windsurfing 12
wrestling 4, 14–15

Zeuner, Brighton 29

Websites

The International Olympic Committee site at **olympic.org** has information about the sports at the Games (click on the SPORTS drag-down menu). Clicking on a sport will take you to the individual events, latest news and sometimes a short video.

At **tokyo2020.org** you can find out the latest about the Tokyo 2020 Games, and at tokyo2020.org/en/games/sport/olympic/ there is information about individual sports, events and venues.

Books to read

The Olympics Ancient to Modern: A Guide to the History of the Games & The Olympics: Going for Gold: A Guide to the Summer Games by Joe Fullman (Wayland, 2015)
Discover Olympic history and events

Olympic Expert by Paul Mason (Franklin Watts, 2016)
A guide to the different events at the Olympics, peppered with fun facts about subjects like the Olympic tug-of-war, the biggest sulk in Olympic history, the 22 minute balancing contest in an Olympic bike race, and much more.